Splatter and Friends

www.splatterandfriends.com

Written and Illustrated by
Melissa Perry Moraja

Melissa Productions, Inc.
www.melissaproductions.com

Thank you Joshua for teaching me about Stranger Danger!

Love,

Mom

Text copyright © 2004 by Melissa Perry Moraja
Illustrations copyright © 2004 by Melissa Perry Moraja
All rights reserved

Published by Melissa Productions, Inc.
www.melissaproductions.com
Printed in the United States

Splatter and Friends: Stranger Danger! Play and Stay Safe
Melissa Perry Moraja.-1st ed.
ISBN 978-0-9842394-4-3

"Today I'm going to teach you what to do when a stranger says that he may know you. Please pay attention to what I say, and in the end, you'll be safe when you play."

Razzle's Stranger Danger Safety Rules

Hi Josh!

Razzle's Stranger Danger Safety Rules

Never go in a stranger's car
even if they know who you are.

Never take a treat
from anyone you just meet.

Always ask for permission
in every proposition.

Never wander off on your own
especially with someone unknown.

"You know the rules now, so let's go play!
The playground is only a few blocks away."

Hooray!

"Please come here!" a lady shouted from the street.
"Your mom said I could take you for a quick bite to eat."

"What should we do?" Josh asked Razzle for advice.
"This lady my mom sent seems to be nice."

"Your mom never told me about any lady.
Let's hurry away. She seems kind of shady."

Stranger Danger!

Next a little old woman offered them a treat.
The candy looked yummy and so sweet to eat.

Josh turned to Razzle not knowing what to do.
"Couldn't I just have one, or maybe two?"

"We don't know this old woman," Razzle said, sounding firm.
"Say, 'No thanks,' and leave to never return."

Stranger Danger!

Suddenly, a man stopped them both in their tracks.
"Please help us find our dog. He's tiny and black.

"These men need our help!" Josh cried out in distress.
"They seem to have gotten themselves in a mess."

"An adult should NEVER ask a kid for help!"
Razzle said to Josh, giving out a loud yelp.

"Stranger Danger! Stranger Danger! Run as fast as you can far away from this potentially dangerous man."

Stranger Danger!

Huffing and puffing they entered the playground.
And immediately began running around.

Josh zoomed to the swings. Razzle stayed by the slide.
No longer did Josh have his friend by his side.

A man walked over and said, "Hi, I'm Jack. Check out my new train. It goes fast on the track!"

"I love playing with trains!" Josh jumped and cheered.
"But I don't know you. Maybe I should stay clear?"

"I have more trains I'm willing to share.
"Just follow me past those bushes right there!"

"What should I do? I don't know this man.
I'll go ask Razzle to see if I can!"

"Razzle, Razzle, can I go with Jack?
He has lots of trains. I promise to come back!"

"NO you can't go with a person I don't know.
No matter if his name is Jack, Mike, or Joe."

"Stranger Danger! Stranger Danger!" Razzle exclaimed.
"I'll call 911. You should be ashamed."

Jack knew he was wrong, so he hurried away.
Now they were safe. Hip Hip Hooray!

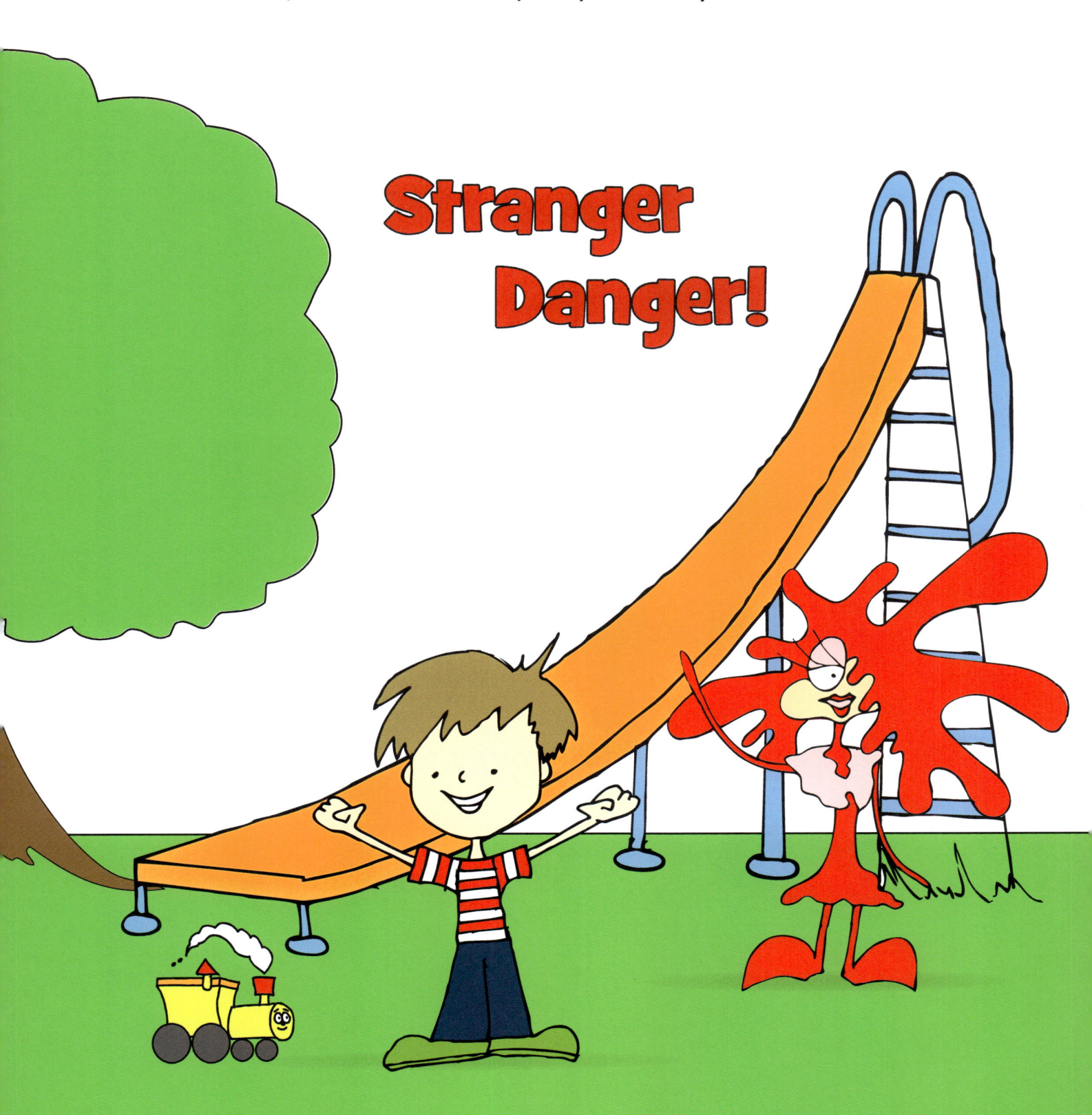

Stranger Danger!

"Before we go, let's review the safety rules.
So you can share them with your friends at school."

Play and stay safe!

Razzle's Stranger Danger Safety Rules

Never go in a stranger's car even if they know who you are.

Never take a treat from anyone you just meet.

Always ask for permission in every proposition.

Never wander off on your own especially with someone unknown.

More beginning reading books your children will love!